Potty Training

The ultimate guide to potty training your child fast and effectively!

Table of Contents

Introduction iv

Chapter 1 – What Is Potty Training? 1

Chapter 2 – When Is the Right Time to Start Potty Training? 5

Chapter 3 – The Basic Steps of Potty Training 12

Chapter 4 – Do's in Potty Training 19

Chapter 5 – Don'ts in Potty Training 24

Chapter 6 – Making Potty Training Fun! 30

Conclusion 39

Introduction

I want to thank you and congratulate you for downloading the book, *"Potty Training"*.

This book contains helpful information about potty training your child. This book will explain to you when you should begin potty training, and how to tell that your child is ready to start learning to use the potty!

Included in this book are a wide range of potty training techniques, each designed to help train your child as fast as possible.

You will learn about the common errors that parents make when potty training their child, and how to best avoid these mistakes.

With the tips and techniques included in this book, you will be able to potty train your child fast, and make it an enjoyable experience for both you and your son or daughter!

I wish you the best of luck, and hope this book is able to help you!

Thanks again for downloading this book, I hope you enjoy it!

Chapter 1 – What Is Potty Training?

Most parents are eager to witness the milestones in their child's development. Regardless if it's their first child or not, for parents, there's no exaggeration to the fact that these milestones must be documented. For them, all their child's "firsts" are newsworthy. Parents will not pass on the opportunity of taking footage or a photo of their child's first bath, first meal, first day out, and the list goes on and on. Think of all the "firsts" that come to mind, most parents are anticipating each and every one of these. Yes, you guessed it right, potty training is one of these developmental milestones.

As defined in Cambridge Dictionary, potty training, also known as toilet training, is the process of teaching a child to use a potty or a toilet. The word "training" refers to the acquisition of skills, knowledge and experience, which in this case is "going to the toilet". There you have it, children in training. This means that they have yet to acquire the necessary skills in going to the potty; thus, they need maximum assistance each step of the way.

Potty training or toilet training is a unique story for every child. It is a journey that you and your child must only embark upon if you are mentally, physically and emotionally ready. This task entails more than just sitting your child on the potty a number of times a day. It takes dedication, patience and hard work! Some children get it right away, while for others, it takes weeks or months. This means very long days of constantly reminding the child to go to the toilet, giving compliments, and cleaning after accidents for the parents and caregivers.

Therefore, when you decide that it's time to potty train your child, make sure to pack lots and lots of patience! You see, potty training doesn't stop when your child is able to sit on the toilet on their own; it's not even when he/she can go on queue because you remind him/her about going to the potty numerous times in a day. These are merely benchmarks where you would see that your child is on the way to being completely "potty trained".

It's a good idea to recognize improvements along your training and to acknowledge your child's efforts. Simple rewards and reinforcements can go a long way! But, as mentioned earlier, a child who is in training needs maximum assistance. Thus, your child must be able to tell when he/she needs to go, sit on the potty, do their business and clean up afterwards all on their own before you can consider them completely "potty trained".

Now, let's look at why it is important to potty train your child. Aside from the obvious reason that changing the diaper every time your child goes is no fun at all, potty training has other benefits that go above and beyond the mere task of going to the potty.

1. **Potty training can be good for your child's health.** First on the list is saying goodbye to those diaper rashes that constantly irritate your child. Next, potty training also lessens the risk of urinary and bowel problems. Studies show that children who are trained later are more likely to develop bladder control problems which may lead to urinary tract infection and reduced muscle control in the pelvic area because they tend to hold their urine and bowel for as long as possible due to their busy schedule, also known as playtime.

2. **Potty training can help parents save money.** Let's admit it, diapers are expensive! And you can't

finish the job with diapers alone! You need wipes, diaper creams, etc. Once your child is potty trained you will automatically cut down on these expenses and be saving more money!

3. **Potty training helps increase your child's self-esteem.** Aside from gaining control over his/her own body, being "potty trained" gives your child a sense of independence and capability. They would feel that they are a "big boy" or a "big girl" now that they can go to the toilet on their own. Consequently, thinking that they are now a "big boy/girl" will make your child more confident to try new things.

4. **Potty training is a way to show love for the environment!** Disposable diapers aren't exactly biodegradable, and so, the more we use them, the more we contribute to pollution. Imagine the pile of diapers that build up in landfills every month and think of how many diapers won't be contributed to that pile if you potty train early. See? Saying goodbye to diapers seems like a small move but it has quite an impact on the environment.

If potty training early gives us a good set of benefits, delaying toilet training can also have some negative effects. As mentioned earlier, it increases the risk of urinary and bowel problems. Another downside of potty training late is that as your child grows, they become more aware and opinionated, making it harder for parents to establish authority. As we all know, sometimes kids enjoy challenging adults with their unbelievable stubbornness.

Now that we're talking about stubbornness, when you potty train late, you risk the possibility that your child may have gotten accustomed to a lazy lifestyle - one where your child is so comfortable wearing a diaper and is too stubborn to stand up to go to the toilet. You see, as time goes, children think that as long as they have their diapers on there is no need to interrupt their playtime. Once they have this kind of thinking, the task of potty training them successfully is prolonged and becomes more difficult.

Potty training or toilet training is a milestone in your child's development. There is a right time for it. Pushing it too early or doing it too late may just result in prolonging the learning process. Open your eyes and be keen with your observations. Your child's behavior and actions may actually be hints that it's time to start potty training!

Chapter 2 – When Is the Right Time to Start Potty Training?

Statistics show that children begin showing signs of readiness for toilet training as early as 18 months up to 3 years of age. Potty training must be approached in a holistic manner as it can be a daunting process. This means that we want the child to be completely ready and up to the task before starting potty training. As we have established earlier, potty training is a unique journey for each child, but in every case, the child's mental, physical and emotional preparedness must be considered. It is understandable that parents tend to be overly excited with this major milestone in their child's development, but this doesn't change the fact that there is a right time to start training. Starting too early or too late will only be counterproductive.

Now if you're wondering whether it's the right time to start potty training or toilet training, start observing your child's routines and behaviors. Ask yourself the following questions.

1. **Does your child recognize when he/she needs to urinate or defecate?**

    Children usually have mannerisms that accompany their need to go, like their facial expression or touching their private area indicating that they need to pee or poop. As they become more aware, children start to show more obvious signs like going to the corner of the room or hiding under the table.

Some children stop what they are doing, stand up and just stay in their spot while they do their thing. Spend time with your child and look for similar hints. This should tell you that your child is becoming more aware about their need to go number one or number two.

2. **Can your child stay dry for 2 hours at a time?**

After a nap or after spending the afternoon playing, check if their nappies are dry. It is important to take note of this as it will show if your child can hold urine in their bladder. Having bladder control is important for your child to reach the potty or the toilet in time without any "accidents".

3. **Can your child follow simple instructions?**

This is very basic since you are preparing to train your child for a new skill. Your child must be able to comprehend and follow simple requests like "Please sit down." or "Stay in your spot." Understanding simple requests and simple questions are crucial for your child to understand the steps that they need to follow.

4. **Can your child pull down or pull up their pants?**

This skill is important for a child to go to the potty on their own, but it proves to be a bit more difficult for younger kids. You can help your child out by scaffolding. Pull the pants up or down a little and let them pull it all the way up or down. This way, your child gets credit for finishing the job - throw in a few positive remarks and your child will be eager try it on their own next time.

5. **Is your child showing interest to use the toilet?**

   Intrinsic motivation is the best kind of motivation. It's best to teach your child new skills when he/she is showing signs that they want to learn that skill. Observe, is your child peeking when adults use the toilet? Does he/she insist on removing their diaper and ask for assistance to try the toilet? If you answered yes, congratulations! Your child is really amused by the toilet! It would be a good idea to take advantage of this amusement. Use your child's curiosity to make their potty training more effective.

Mental preparedness means that your child must be ready to understand and absorb this new skill set. As emphasized in item number 3, your child must be able to hear out simple instructions and follow through. This is important in establishing a new routine. "Understanding" does not refer to simply following the instruction given; rather, the child must be able to recall and follow the same instructions the next time a similar incident occurs. For example, "Stay in your spot when eating." This is a simple yet tricky request as kids struggle with staying in their spot especially with playmates or toys around.

A child may hear your request and follow without actually understanding it. You will observe that your child will stay in his/her spot longer when eating the more that they understand the routine. Understanding goes hand in hand with your child's attention span. The more they understand your instruction, the more they will try to stay focused on the task at hand. The key is consistency. Developing your child's understanding and attention span is not a one day process, but if you are consistent your child is sure to show progress. Make sure that your child is advancing in these areas before you start potty training because explaining new routines and why they need to use the toilet will be a struggle if your child is still all about playing.

Physical preparedness refers to your child's control over their body. Initially, you have to observe your child's fine motor skills and gross motor skills. This refers to the small and big movements that your child can do. Can your child hold small objects firmly? Can your child stand, sit and walk on their own? Fine motor skills and gross motor skills are important in potty training. For example, standing up, walking to the potty and sitting on the potty all requires gross motor skills, while pulling their pants up or down requires both fine and gross motor skills. Another factor that you must consider in determining your child's physical preparedness is showing awareness of their body. As emphasized in item number 1, before potty training, it is important that the child can recognize when they need to urinate or have a bowel movement.

Emotional preparedness means that your child is up to the task and is not pressured to start potty training. You must understand that starting potty training will be a major change in your child's routines, thus, doing this alongside other major changes like a new school or a new caregiver may overwhelm your child and hence cause setbacks in your toilet training. To avoid such setbacks it is important that you plan ahead of time. Consider upcoming changes like moving to a new house or having new people around in deciding when to start potty training.

Once you have picked the date, ensure that your child is emotionally up to the task by gradually mentioning the upcoming change, which in this case is potty training. Occasionally mention how he/she is now a "big boy" or a "big girl" and that big kids use the potty. You may also show your child pictures of toilet seats and potties ahead of time, preferably colorful ones. This way, instead of being scared and overwhelmed, your child might actually be excited to get started!

Once you have seen that your child is mentally, physically and emotionally ready, then it's time to step back and take a look at yourself. Are you ready to start this journey with your child? Some parents focus so much on how ready their child is and forget to consider whether or not they themselves are ready to potty train their kids. Again, potty training is not as simple as sitting your child on the potty. When you start training, you need to be dedicated. You have to allot portions of your day for potty training alone. You'll be investing in equipment like a toilet seat, a potty and possible rewards and innovative tools which you may use to reinforce your child's learning. Not to mention the "accidents" which are bound to happen and can be frustrating.

You see, aside from the actual potty training part, there's the cleaning part where you act like a detective and make sure that the "accident" didn't leave any evidence on the furniture or on the floor. Potty training your toddler is no joke, it entails plenty of hard work and tons of patience. Make sure that you are also mentally, physically and emotionally ready for all the ups and downs before deciding to jump into potty training.

Mental preparedness is important, especially for new parents. Read about potty training or toilet training for there is no better tool than knowledge. Research as much as you can about potty training and learn about all your options in training your child. No one knows your child better than you. Observe your child's behaviors and capacities, and based on these you may choose potty training techniques that will work for both of you. After all, potty training goes differently for each child. What worked for your elder child or your neighbor's child may not work for the one you will be training.

Physical preparedness means you are healthy and fit to potty train your child. Remember, in the potty training scenario, you are the trainer! You would want to start training your child when you're at the peak of your physical health. Ensure that you have enough rest and that you do not have other physical stressors like excessive amounts of work. Potty training includes a lot of physical work from assisting your child in going to the potty, getting him/her to stay on the potty, and of course cleaning up which as we all know is never easy. Being the trainer, you want to be able to give your full focus and energy to completing the task.

Emotional preparedness for the parents means setting realistic goals and understanding that each child's potty training journey is unique. Before starting potty training your child, you must understand with your mind and soul that "accidents" will happen. Yes, potty training can be a very frustrating and emotional journey for parents, and you must accept that before starting. Otherwise, you might end up pressuring yourself or your child to get the job done as soon as possible. Society also adds pressure to this emotional knapsack.

For example, when you hear that your neighbor's child or your child's classmate at preschool, who is of the same age as yours, is now potty trained, you may end up comparing and wondering where you went wrong. Don't fret it! As we have established, potty training is not a one day process and the length of training will vary for each child.

Potty training or toilet training is a major milestone. There is a right time for it, and the right time is different for each child. Don't let society dictate what's best for your child! You know your child better and you know his/her capabilities. If you think that it's your little one's time to shine, step back and assess your child's readiness and yours. If all the signs are telling you that you are both mentally, physically and emotionally prepared then there is no doubt that you are ready to start potty training!

Chapter 3 – The Basic Steps of Potty Training

In potty training your child, you are the trainer. And as the trainer, you must understand the elements of potty training. As mentioned, potty training must be approached in a holistic manner, thus, you must have a clear vision of what you want to achieve and how you plan to achieve it. To help you out in planning your child's special journey, here are the basic steps of potty training:

1. **Asses your child's and your own readiness.**

   Do not force potty training just because your neighbor's child is already potty trained. The timeline for potty training is unique for each child and is different for boys and girls. Start potty training when you and your child are both ready and not for any other reason. There's absolutely no need to push it if you are not a hundred percent ready. Trying to potty train too early or too late will only compromise your progress and result in a prolonged time table. Mental, physical and emotional preparedness is important!

   As discussed in the previous chapter, watch out for signs like your child's ability to walk, sit and stand or their ability to follow instructions. These signs should tell you that your child is ready. Once your child is ready, don't jump into potty training just because they're already there. Ensure that you are also a hundred percent ready because you are the trainer and your child will need you each step of the way.

2. **Mentally prepare your child for potty training.**

   Gradually introduce the idea of potty training to your child. Constantly remind him/her that he/she is now a "big boy" or a "big girl" and that big kids do things a little differently and they are obedient. Visual is also important. When your child poops, show them how big the poop is. Use phrases like "your poop is getting too big for the diaper" or "soon you will try to poop in the potty". You may also try laying low on the diapers and let your child wear undies from time to time, explaining that "big boys" or "big girls" wear undies instead of diapers. This way, your child will not be overwhelmed by sudden changes when you start potty training because subconsciously they were already expecting the change in their routine.

3. **Buy a potty chair or an adapter seat that your child will love!**

   Take note, something "that your child will love". This is important, remember that potty training may take up a lengthy period of time and throughout that time, their potty will be their best friend. Therefore it's a good idea to include your child in deciding which potty or adapter seat will be perfect for them. Some kids tend to be scared of the appearance of the adult toilet. If your child is one of these kids, a special adapter seat would be a good idea to help them get acquainted with the adult toilet. But if this is too much for your child, there's no rush in sitting them on the adult toilet. You can always get a cute potty chair that your child would find fun.

4. **Plan a routine for your child.**

   Now that you have a potty chair, it's time that you let your child get familiar with it. Starting with once a day, let your child sit on the potty chair, even with clothes on. This may be done after breakfast of after a nap. Once you have picked the right time for your child to sit on the potty, be consistent. Just let your child get comfortable with sitting on the potty chair. The goal is simply to let your child recognize the potty chair as a part of their daily routine. If you tried this with clothes on first, once your child is comfortable with the potty chair, gradually adjust to sitting them on the potty with a bare bottom.

5. **Learning through imitation.**

   All children learn by copying. In this step, some families imply the "open door policy" at home. This means that whenever adults need to pee they leave the door open so that the toddler may see how girls and boys use the toilet. Naturally, the child will be curious and will ask questions. This then, gives the parents the opportunity to explain the difference between boys and girls when they use the toilet. Other families prefer the "one-on-one method" where if the child is a boy, daddy or any adult male figure would let him watch when he uses the toilet.

   On the other hand if the child is a girl, mommy or any adult female figure would let her watch when she uses the toilet. What's important in this step is for the child to see how he/she is supposed to use potty. As mentioned earlier, the visuals are important. Children mirror what they see adults doing. And because of their curious nature, children are likely to try sitting on the potty chair on their own after seeing adults on the toilet.

6. **Explain how to go to the potty**.

   You have introduced the idea. You have bought the equipment. And you have demonstrated the procedure. Now is the time for you to explain what you have been doing all along. When your child poops, bring them to the toilet and drop the poop beneath while he is seated. Clean up and then flush the toilet. Some children will delight in flushing the toilet themselves and watching their poop go down. While others, those who are sensitive to change, will most likely be scared at first and just prefer to watch you do it.

   After doing this routine a couple of times, your child will understand that poop is supposed to go down the toilet. You may also want to reinforce your child's understanding and recall of the potty process by using story books and posters about potty training. Through these your child may have a better understanding of why he/she needs to use the potty and memorizing the steps would definitely be easier if they are presented in a story or via pictures, as young kids are often visual learners.

7. **Reinforcing the habit**.

   Now that your little one is familiar with the process of going to the potty, constant reminders and encouragements are necessary. As they say, the key is consistency. Remind your child to go to the potty every time he/she feels the need to go. And when your child goes to the potty, make sure to keep them company. This will help your child ease in to the process and it will keep them focused on the task at hand. Let your child sit on the potty for a few minutes. If you're not lucky, it's okay. Try again in 15 minutes or 30 minutes. Constantly asking your child if they need to go is another effective technique.

During this stage, some parents let their children play with bare bottoms. Why? Because then they would be out of the diaper and there's nothing to catch their pee or poop. Once they realize what a mess it makes, kids seek out the potty. However, this is not a one day process. If you decide to try this technique, be prepared to clean puddles of pee here and there.

In the interest of reinforcing the habit of using the potty, make sure to shower your child with praises whenever they successfully use the potty or succeeds in having an "accident" free day. Simple rewards also work great with most kids. This can vary from small toys, story books, or art materials, whatever works for your child. When you do this, your child will feel that they did something great! The more positive reinforcement a child receives, the more likely it is for them to repeat the reinforced behavior.

8. **Accepting "accidents"**.

As your child goes through potty training, they will grow more and more independent. By now, your child can probably go to the potty with minimum assistance. Maybe you just need to constantly ask your child if they need to go, or maybe you need to help them pull down or pull up their pants. As long as they need your assistance at some point of the routine, then they are yet to be considered "potty trained". Therefore, even if you have achieved a series of "accident" free days, they may still happen. And if they do happen, handle them with grace. Setbacks happen, remember, your child is learning a new skill set.

Don't scold your child for making a mess, instead acknowledge the parts of the routine that they did accomplish. For example, if your child's playing when they felt the need to go and they did try to go to the potty but did not make it, acknowledge the fact that your child tried to go to the potty. This means that they remembered the routine, appreciate that. Use encouragements like, "It's okay, next time we'll walk faster to reach the potty".

9. **Night training.**

It's normal for children to wet their bed occasionally until they're of school age. And so, it's a good idea to continue letting your toddler wear diapers at night time. However, do keep your child's potty chair near his/her bed. This way, just like with daytime potty training, you can constantly encourage your child that if he/she happens to wake up in the middle of the night and feels the need to go, he/she can call your attention and ask for assistance to use the potty.

When you notice that your child can stay consistently dry at night, then you may try to do away with the diaper. But before you embark on diaper free nights there are a few things that you might want to consider. First on the list is protecting your mattress from possible "accidents", a good hack for this dilemma would be to wrap the mattress with plastic before you put the bed sheet on. Once your bed is secured, it's time to prepare your child for his/her diaper free night.

To lessen the risk of bed wetting most parents lay off milk at least an hour before bedtime. Less fluids means less chance of needing to pee in the middle of the night. They also let their child use the toilet before bedtime and first thing in the morning. This technique works because instead of needing to wake up just to use the potty the child's body is conditioned to release excess fluid before bedtime and upon waking up. This will work for the best, since your child has already mastered daytime potty use.

Children usually master daytime potty training before they are ready to start night time potty training. Now, when can you say that your child is "completely potty trained"? You see, during potty training, a child constantly needs to be reminded to use the potty. When still training, the child needs company and hand over hand assistance every now and then. Once you are confident that your child can recognize when they need to use the potty without being reminded and that they can get the job done without any help whatsoever, regardless if it's daytime or night time, congratulations! Your child can be considered "potty trained".

Chapter 4 – Do's in Potty Training

In any kind of training, it is important that everything you do aims for progress and results. And because potty training is different for every child, you must figure out what works best for your child. You already know the basic steps of potty training your child, now let's tackle a list of "do's" that you may follow throughout your training period.

DO make sure that your child is a hundred percent ready to embark on the potty training journey. This means that the child should have mental, physical and emotional preparedness as discussed in the previous chapters.

DO plan things ahead of time. Things are always easier when done in an organized fashion. Decide when you want to start potty training and carefully plan how you want to achieve your goal. Consider all variables that may impact your child's learning. This includes your child's readiness, your schedule, equipment that you may need and other tools that may reinforce learning.

DO take note of your child's natural elimination routine. Observe what time your child usually pees or poops during the day and write it down. Do this at least a week before you start potty training, this will help you in planning a potty schedule for your child.

DO get people involved in the potty training process. You see, potty training a child can be a daunting task. Thus, it's not a job for a one-man team. Both parents need to be hands-on in training the child. In fact, all members of the family can play a role in the training process. Constant reminders, encouragements and praises will have a more positive effect on the child if everyone is consistent. If your child goes to a daycare and/or a preschool, it would be for the best if you inform the caregivers and/or teachers that you are potty training. Inform them of the strategies that you are using so that they may do the same whenever your child is with them.

DO make a potty schedule for your child. Based on the natural elimination routine that you have written down, decide which parts of the day are best for potty training your child. This can be every morning, after naps, after eating and so on. It really depends on your child's default routine. Why? Because it will be easier to potty train your child in times of the day when they usually pees or poops rather than forcing them to sit on the potty randomly during the day.

DO break the process into simple steps. This is essential, especially if your child is responding negatively, resisting, or is scared of the toilet. Do things one step at a time. Just like in the steps discussed in the previous chapter, sit your child on the potty or on the toilet with clothes on first. Once they are used to it, then you can try sitting them on the potty or on the toilet with bare bottoms. Always introduce new steps in a gradual manner. This way, you can avoid overwhelming your child or making them feel pressured.

DO remind your child to use the potty at constant intervals. Once your child is comfortable sitting on the potty chair following their potty schedule, you may start increasing their potty chair time. This can be every 15 minutes, every 30 minutes, or every hour, whichever is closer to your child's regular eliminating routine. Many parents use alarms to make sure that they stick to their schedule. Some even give their kids watches with alarms that buzz. This way the kids can be more involved and they can take the initiative to stop what they are doing because it's time to sit on the potty chair.

DO make it fun. Potty training or toilet training can be a long and exhausting process for you and your child. And just like at work or at school, the difficulty of any task triples if you are not enjoying what you are doing. And so, find simple ways to make potty training enjoyable for you and your child. Try watching a movie while having potty time!

DO use motivating tools. Read a story or sing a song about potty training. You may also use pictures or posters. Be innovative in motivating your child to use the potty! Positive reinforcement always goes a long way. Simple rewards like a piece of chocolate or a cookie each time your child uses the potty will keep him/her motivated.

DO praise your child for his/her efforts. Aside from physical rewards, verbal praises can do magic in keeping your child motivated. Children are always proud when they accomplish something and this is how they will feel every time you acknowledge their efforts. Not only will verbal praises motivate your child to stick to his/her potty training routine, it will also boost their confidence and sense of independence.

DO accept that "accidents" will happen. Since your child is undergoing training, you can't exactly expect dryness 24/7. Accidents are bound to happen. These are just temporary setbacks and having an "accident" doesn't mean that your potty training is a failure. Acknowledge your child's efforts and encourage him/her to get to the potty faster next time. As the saying goes, try and try until you succeed.

DO let your child be involved in cleaning up. Give your child simple tasks when cleaning up after an "accident". Maybe just putting his/her clothes in the hamper or handing you a rug. In doing this, your child will feel independent and all grown up. He/she becomes aware that it's not easy to clean up, thus, he/she will be more careful to avoid accidents next time. By practicing this, you are also teaching your child to be responsible and neat.

DO stay calm when potty training your child. It is perfectly understandable if at some point you feel frustrated about the progress in your child's potty training. Breathe in! Breathe out! Always keep in mind that each child's potty training timetable is different. Avoid comparing your child's progress with those of other children's, you will only feel pressured. Don't be hard on yourself and on your child! Look at potty training as a unique journey for you and your child, savor every moment of it and just enjoy witnessing your child's progress. Remember, patience is a virtue.

DO ask older kids to be an example for your child in training. If you haven't noticed, toddlers love to copy older kids. And so if you ask an older kid (preferably 4 or 5 years old) to demonstrate the proper use of the potty, copying them will be second nature to your toddler.

DO bring a portable potty whenever you leave the house. As your kid has not mastered bladder control yet, he/she may make sudden announcements about the need to go in the middle of your trip. You wouldn't want to be caught off guard, now would you? You see, even if your destination has a restroom, sometimes it's just too far to avoid accidents!

DO celebrate once your child is completely potty trained. After all the hard work that you and your child have put into potty training, a celebration is in order! Make sure to acknowledge your child's achievement and don't forget to give yourself a pat on the back too! You can go out for ice cream, or make a special treat at home to reward your child. You can have a lunch out or dinner out with the whole family. There are plenty of ways to celebrate the milestone that you and your child just conquered! It doesn't have to be grand, but it needs to be fun!

Chapter 5 – Don'ts in Potty Training

If there are things that are highly recommended when potty training a child, of course there are also things that are highly discouraged. No matter how daunting and frustrating the potty training process is, it is highly advised for you, the trainer, not to get carried away with your emotions. Your child needs you to complete this major milestone, thus you need to keep your head in the game! To keep you guided, here are some of the don'ts when potty training a child:

DON'T start potty training if your child is not ready. As discussed in the previous chapters, mental, physical and emotional preparedness must be attained by the child before you start potty training. This means that they can recognize when they need to pee, they can walk, sit and stand on their own, and so on. Forcing your child to learn something that they are not ready for may only upset them and cause delays in the learning process.

Even if the child shows readiness in many ways, observe their initial response to potty training. Are they excited or upset? The child's behavior may be an indication that they're not yet one hundred percent ready. Maybe they're overwhelmed by the size of the adult toilet, maybe they are just hungry or maybe you are coming on too strong. Regardless of the reason, if your child is too upset to start training it's okay to postpone starting the training by a few hours, a few days or a few weeks.

DON'T pressure your child or yourself. Allow your child to follow their natural pace and just let them ease in to your potty training routine. There is no standard timetable for potty training and as pointed out in previous chapters this is a unique journey for each child. And so, to keep from pressuring your child or yourself, just let things flow naturally and avoid comparing your child's progress with those of other kid's. Your kid's pace is different from theirs, and that's not a bad thing!

DON'T shoulder the burden all by yourself. It may seem easy at first but when the exhaustion and frustration kicks in, you'll need someone by your side. Even superheroes need help sometimes! Asking for help is not a sign of weakness. Rather, it's a sign of strength! It shows that your family can work as a team to achieve a common goal!

DON'T turn potty training into a battle of wills. You and your child are on the same team although you may not feel this, especially when your child throws tantrums. Major changes tend to overwhelm and upset children in the beginning but they'll eventually ease into the change. If ever your child is upset, just remain calm but be firm in giving instructions. Make sure that they follow through with your request even after throwing tantrums. Remind them of the rewards, if you prepared any, like a piece of chocolate or a cookie if they complete the task.

DON'T let your child wear pants that are too tight or difficult to remove. As a part of potty training, you want your child to be able to pull their pants down or up all on their own. However, this task can be close to impossible if your child is wearing clothes that are too tight or have too many buttons, zippers, etc.

DON'T overreact. Yes, you need to give your child positive reinforcements and constant praises, but don't overdo it! You don't need to have a parade or throw a party every time your kid uses the potty. You may do a dance or sing songs if these are part of your techniques. Sometimes, a simple acknowledgement like "Good job! You are really growing up!" will do.

DON'T scold your child whenever he/she has "accidents" or refuses to follow your potty training routine. Getting angry will not accomplish anything. If anything, it will only turn potty training into a negative experience for your child and lessen their interest to continue training. And so, whenever you encounter setbacks, try your best to address it calmly.

Focus on the achievement rather than the accident. Did your child tell you that he/she needs to use the potty? Did they try to go to the potty? Appreciate and acknowledge the things that your kid does try to do even if they did not actually make it to the potty.

DON'T give in to tantrums. In the middle of potty training some kids regress and suddenly feel overwhelmed by the changes. During this period, the child is very likely to throw tantrums and demand diapers back as it is easier for them that way. Don't give in! We know that sometimes it is dead hard to resist those teary eyes, rounded cheeks, and pouted lips, but get a hold of yourself! Giving in to the cuteness won't help either. If you do give in, you will only nurture the negative behavior, start an endless cycle of tantrums, and cause further setbacks in your potty training.

The incessant crying, kicking on the floor and probable throwing of things can be unbearable at times, however, keep in mind that this is just a phase. When your child calms down, remind them why they need to use the potty. Reinforce this by relating their experience with those in potty training story books or remind them of the reward that you promised once they are completely potty trained.

DON'T expect your child to meet a deadline. Yes, some children can get the job done in just a matter of days but it doesn't mean that your child can do it just the same. Each child follows a unique timetable. This means that your child too can get the job done in their own time. Besides, if you set a deadline, you will only be putting pressure on you and your child. And putting pressure can only result in frustration and exhaustion.

DON'T stick to one technique only. Potty training can be a trial and error process because each child is unique. In the beginning it may be tricky for some parents to figure out the best technique/s for their child. You see, in teaching or training, there is no "one" perfect technique to ensure learning. This is why you may always try one, two, three or more techniques simultaneously until you find the right mix of techniques for your child's unique journey. It won't hurt to explore other options if your child's progress in potty training is taking a long time, or if the new technique that you found can boost your child's learning. In the end, make sure to be consistent in implementing rules on the techniques that you have chosen because no matter how great the techniques are, if you cannot deliver them properly it will be difficult to get positive results.

DON'T be afraid to innovate. There are plenty of tricks to make potty training fun, but if you can't find the right trick for your child, it's okay. Maybe the perfect technique for your child is hiding in plain sight. Perhaps it has something to do with your pet dog, their favorite food, or favorite movie. If you are still not satisfied, try mixing a few tricks together and coming up with a unique trick which is fit with your child's learning style.

DON'T make the child wait when he/she tells you that he needs to go. Young kids don't have full bladder control. Therefore when your child tells you that they need to go, it means that they need to go right away! Delays may only result in "accidents". Also, if your child gets used to holding their pee or poop in, the risks of urinary tract infection and constipation become real. This is why you should always keep a portable potty near your child's area at home and you should also have one with you when you are leaving the house with your toddler.

DON'T broadcast your child's mishaps. This is especially true if your child is within earshot. Hearing you joke off with your friends about their "accidents" may affect their motivation and interest in potty training. Besides, if your child is in their talkative phase, they will likely tell stories of funny incidents.

DON'T go back to diapers! Once you have introduced big kid undies and once your child is used to it, that's it! Even if they occasionally wet themselves, don't go back to diapers! Clean up the "accident" and go about your normal routine. Yes, it can be frustrating to clean up after pee puddles just when you thought your kid was finally potty trained, and during such scenarios it is very tempting to grab a diaper and put it on your child. However, doing this will only confuse your child and may even cause regression. Don't let all your efforts go to waste by giving in to the comfort that the diaper offers. Stays focused and just keep reinforcing the potty habit that your child is slowly developing.

DON'T panic whenever you encounter setbacks. Even after a few days or weeks of total dryness, there can still be occasional "accidents". This is okay. Just because your little one accidentally wets themselves doesn't mean you have to go back to square one. Take a deep breath! There's no need to panic. Perhaps your child is just so engrossed with their activity that they forgot to go to the potty. As discussed in the previous chapter, handle accidents with grace. Calmly remind your child to go to the potty next time and then because they are already a "big kid" ask them to help you out in cleaning. Kids love to be involved in grown up activities, plus helping cleanup will remind them to be more careful next time.

Chapter 6 – Making Potty Training Fun!

Young children are visual learners - they like colorful toys, colorful pictures, colorful story books and so on. You can use this trait to your advantage in the potty training process by innovating and being creative with your reinforcements. But as we all know, there are multiple types of intelligence, and as early as 2 years old you can probably see some signs of which intelligence your child is inclined to. Ask yourself what your child is interested in. Is it music? Is it arts and crafts? Whatever your child's interests are, you can always find a way to use it to your advantage. Innovate, be creative, and make potty training fun! Here are a few creative ideas that you may try with your child:

1. **Potty Scrapbook.**

    This is fun for both the parent and the child! Furthermore, it's a creative way of documenting your child's potty training progress. Buy a pre-made scrapbook or make one from scratch and then fill the pages with your child's potty training achievements. You can compile pictures in your child's journey, and add the receipts of the potty training equipment that you bought. Anything goes! Show the scrapbook to your child and work with them whenever you're putting entries in the scrapbook. This is a great art activity for kids and it gets them excited, knowing that they'll have an art project every time they have little potty achievements.

2. **Design your potty project.**

   Have your child claim the potty chair as their own! Once you have bought the perfect potty chair for your child, let them play with it. This will make them more comfortable around the potty. Buy some stickers, some stamps, or simply use colored markers and let your child design their potty chair as he/she pleases. Being the designer of such a fabulous potty, your child will surely be excited to try sitting on their masterpiece!

3. **Reading potty books.**

   There are books about potty training that can be perfect for your child. Aside from making potty training fun, these books can help your child understand potty training better as he/she can relate the events in the story with what they're doing. However, potty books don't necessarily have to be a story about potty training. You and your child can have a trip to a local book store and you can let them pick books that they will love.

   Once you have selected your child's potty book/s, explain to them that these are special books that they can only read whenever they're sitting on the potty. This way, the books will also serve as tools to keep your child focused while having their potty time.

4. **Singing potty training songs.**

   When it comes to potty training songs, there are plenty available on the internet. You can just browse for songs that your child would enjoy and then sing it together every time your child uses the potty. You can also make your personalized potty song which may include your child's name and sing it to the tune of famous nursery rhymes. Your child will love this unique touch and will surely feel special hearing their own name in the song.

5. **The potty dance.**

Find simple dance routines online or simply come up with your own simple dance. This will be your child's potty dance or victory dance! You and other members of the family may do this dance along with the child in training every time they successfully use the potty or the toilet. Dancing is fun for kids and calling it a "victory dance" will give your child a sense of achievement every time they get to do the dance. Plus having multiple members of the family do the dance with him/her makes the victory dance even more glorified!

6. **Wearing a potty watch.**

Setting a timer or an alarm is a common technique in potty training. The "potty watch" can be any kiddie watch that has an alarm feature. When potty training, let your child wear their special potty watch and explain that when they hear it beep, it means that they need to sit on his potty chair. When the alarm goes off and after their potty time, the tendency will be for your child to wait for the next beep. Aside from enjoying their new watch and enjoying the beeping sound, this method helps your child to take ownership of their potty routine, of course still with your supervision.

7. **The potty chart.**

   There are plenty of printable potty charts on the internet. Print a few copies and stick it on the wall near the bathroom. Have your child mark or color a square for each day that they are successful in their potty training. Maybe promise a simple reward that your child will love as soon as they mark all the squares.

8. **Bring a potty buddy.**

   Some children are easily overwhelmed by changes in their routine. To make the transition easier for your child, allow them to bring his/her favorite stuffed toy or doll. Use phrases like "your buddy is very brave and you are brave too". This should make your child less anxious about sitting on the potty chair. Some children would prefer to bring their comfort items like their blanket or a favorite toy, this is okay too as long as your child will sit on the potty.

9. **The target practice technique.**

   This technique is especially for boys. Drop some chips or cereals, preferably colorful ones, in the potty or in the toilet. Then explain to your child that in this game he needs to target the pieces of chips or cereals. Little boys will enjoy this game and it really helps with their accuracy.

10. **The magic toilet.**

    For this technique you will need red or blue food colorings. Sprinkle some food color in the water so that when your child pees, the color changes into orange or green. Kids are amazed by this trick as it makes them feel like magicians!

11. The mystery box.

For this technique, you need to buy random inexpensive reward items. You can have small toys, chocolates, candies or art materials, whatever will work for your child.

Once you have your rewards, find an old shoe box and cut a round shaped hole on one side. Make sure your rewards fit in the hole. After this, get a black garbage bag and cut a piece that is big enough to cover the hole in your box. Tape it on the inside of the box so that it covers the hole like a flap from the inside. Wrap your box with attractive gift wrappers and decorate it as you please. When you are satisfied with your mystery box, put the reward items that you prepared inside.

Now, every time that your child successfully uses the potty, they can pick a reward through the hole in the box without any clue as to what items are inside the box. This element of surprise can be mind-blowing for kids! The idea of getting random surprises from a mystery box is sure to keep your child interested in potty training.

12. Sweet treats.

Who can say no to sweet treats? Kids love chocolates, candies, cookies and they'll surely go crazy about any sweet treat that you'll offer them! This is a very easy trick! Simply give your child a piece of chocolate, candy or a cookie every time he/she uses the potty successfully.

13. Stickers.

Kids love attractive stickers! You can use this for an innovative potty chart or simply for an art activity that your kid will love. Bring your child with you when you buy stickers and let him/her choose the design that they love. It would be great if you can find stickers of their favorite characters. Stick a colored paper near the bathroom and have your child put one sticker for each time that they use the potty. Children will enjoy filling the paper with lots of stickers!

To use stickers as an innovative potty chart, assign a colored paper for each skill that you want to keep tabs on. For example, red paper every time your child successfully uses the potty to pee, and blue paper for a successful poop. You can also keep count of other skills like successfully pulling their pants up or down. Label each paper according to the target skills and find a place near the bathroom where you can stick the colored papers. Every time that your child performs the target task successfully, have them pick a sticker and stick it on the appropriate colored paper. This way you can monitor which skills your child is advancing in, depending on the number of stickers on each paper. And just like with a regular potty chart, you may also promise your child a treat or a simple reward whenever they fill out the entire paper.

14. **Stamps.**

Stamps are famous reward tools in preschools and daycares. Why? Because they're cheap and they work! Therefore it can also be a great tool to reward your child when potty training.

Children love to see stamps on their hands. However, you wouldn't want to fill their entire arm with stamps if they use the potty five times in a day, now would you? A good trick here would be to put the stamps on a sheet of paper. Have an agreement with your child that you will only put the third stamp or the fifth stamp on their hand, and that the others will have to go on the paper. This way they will still see the stamp, the mark of their accomplishment and their hands won't end up looking messy.

Another use of stamps would be an innovative potty chart just like the one with the stickers. You can follow the same steps except this time you will be using stamps.

15. **The potty clap.**

Have you ever heard of special reward claps? These are special claps that are usually used in preschool to reinforce children whenever they do something right. Ask a preschool teacher or a caregiver from your child's daycare if they know any special claps. If they don't, you can always search for videos online! Just like the potty dance, you can do the potty clap with your child after they use the potty or the toilet successfully. These claps can be very motivating for children! Kids especially love claps which include stomping every once in a while. Examples of special claps are the wow clap, the firecracker clap, the yes clap, the hamburger clap and so on.

16. **Color when you potty.**

Children love coloring books and activity books! Designate a special coloring book for potty training and allow your child to color one page every time they use the potty successfully.

17. The potty trainer.

Have you ever heard of drink and wet dolls? You can also use them for potty training your child. Once you have purchased the doll, have your child take care of it. Explain to them that they need to potty train the doll just like how you are potty training him/her. Every time the doll gets wet, your child must let it sit on the potty. Children will love the idea of training the doll because this puts them in control and it makes them feel grown up as they are doing the task that mommy and daddy are doing. Furthermore, to be able to potty train the doll they must understand the potty routine themselves. And so, without them realizing it, the more that they train the doll, the more they master their own potty routine!

18. The trophy.

Everyone enjoys rewards and prizes, especially kids! Aside from the sweets, stickers, stamps, etc. which you may give your child "during" potty training, it's a great idea to have a grand prize that your child can look forward to. This can be a craft trophy which you can do as an art project with your child. You can also choose a special toy that your child has been asking you to buy.

Show the trophy or the special toy to your child before you begin potty training. Have him/her take a good look at the prize and admire it for a while. Take note that if it's a toy, they must not open it. This should get them excited to claim it. After a few minutes, explain to your child that this is their prepared trophy! Make sure that your child understands that the trophy belongs to them but they may only get it or open it once they are completely potty trained.

Put the trophy in a place where your child can constantly see it but cannot reach it. Seeing their trophy constantly will remind your child of what he/she is working to achieve, and this will keep them focused on potty training.

These are just a few tricks on how to make potty training fun for you and your child. Some of these may work with your child and some may not. It's a trial and error process.

Truth be told, if you just observe your child's interests and take a good look around your house, there are plenty of ways to make potty training fun! You can use anything that your child loves! This can be a favorite toy or a favorite song. Who knows, Maybe you will even come up with new and unique potty training games! If you think that something can help you to reinforce your child's learning, do it! Find the right mix of techniques and feel free to innovate.

Conclusion

Thank you again for downloading this book!

I hope this book was able to help you learn more about how to potty train your child, and I wish you and your child the best of luck!

Finally, if you enjoyed this book, please take the time to share your thoughts and post a review on Amazon. It'd be greatly appreciated!

Thank you and good luck!

www.ingramcontent.com/pod-product-compliance
Lightning Source LLC
LaVergne TN
LVHW021742060526
838200LV00052B/3427